IMAGES OF WAR SPECIAL
THE GERMAN ARMY
From Mobilisation to First Ypres

RARE PHOTOGRAPHS FROM WARTIME ARCHIVES

OTTO SCHWINK

Pen & Sword
MILITARY

First published in this format in Great Britain in 2016 by
Pen & Sword Military
An imprint of
Pen & Sword Books Ltd
47 Church Street
Barnsley
South Yorkshire
S70 2AS

Copyright © History Copyrights Agency, 2016

ISBN 978 1 47383 780 5

The right of Bob Carruthers to be identified as Author of this work has been asserted by him in accordance with the Copyright, Designs and Patents Act 1988.

A CIP catalogue record for this book is available from the British Library.

All rights reserved. No part of this book may be reproduced or transmitted in any form or by any means, electronic or mechanical including photocopying, recording or by any information storage and retrieval system, without permission from the Publisher in writing.

Printed and bound in England by
By CPI Group (UK) Ltd, Croydon, CR0 4YY

Pen & Sword Books Ltd incorporates the Imprints of Aviation, Atlas, Family History, Fiction, Maritime, Military, Discovery, Politics, History, Archaeology, Select, Wharncliffe Local History, Wharncliffe True Crime, Military Classics, Wharncliffe Transport, Leo Cooper, The Praetorian Press, Remember When, Seaforth Publishing and Frontline Publishing.

For a complete list of Pen & Sword titles please contact
PEN & SWORD BOOKS LIMITED
47 Church Street, Barnsley, South Yorkshire, S70 2AS, England
E-mail: enquiries@pen-and-sword.co.uk
Website: www.pen-and-sword.co.uk

Contents

Introduction 4

Chapter 1   The Road to Ypres 14

Chapter 2   The Race to the Sea 46

Chapter 3   Lille, Antwerp and Beyond 58

Chapter 4   The First Battle of Ypres 80

Chapter 5   The Christmas Truce 84

Chapter 6   The Theatre of Operations 92

Chapter 7   The British Response 102

Chapter 8   Adolf Hitler at Ypres 114

Introduction

In the autumn of 1917 Captain Otto Schwink, a General Staff Officer, by order of the Chief of the General Staff of the Field Army produced a book entitled *The Germans at Ypres 1914*. That work was founded on official documents and the book featured the following preface sanctioned by the General Staff of the Field Army at German Headquarters in the autumn of 1917:

'The gigantic scale of the present war defies comparison with those of the past, and battles which formerly held the world in suspense are now almost forgotten. The German people have been kept informed of the progress of events on all fronts since the 4th August 1914, by the daily official reports of the German General Staff, but the general public will have been unable to gather from these a coherent and continuous story of the operations.

For this reason the General Staff of the German Field Army has decided to permit the publication of a series of monographs which will give the German people a general knowledge of the course of the most important operations in this colossal struggle of nations.

These monographs cannot be called histories of the war; years, even decades, must pass before all the true inwardness and connection of events will be completely revealed. This can only be done when the archives of our opponents have been opened to the world as well as our own and those of the General Staffs of our Allies. In the meantime the German people will be given descriptions of the most important of the battles, written by men who took part in them, and have had the official records at their disposal.

It is possible that later research may make alterations here and there necessary, but this appears no reason for delaying publications based on official documents, indeed to do so would only serve to foster the legends and rumours which so easily take hold of the popular imagination and are so difficult, if not impossible, to correct afterwards.'

Herr Schwink opened his account with a misty eyed recollection of the days of August 1914 when the Imperial German Army was still imbued with the concept of war as a chivalrous game:

'Whoever has lived through those great days of August 1914, and witnessed the wonderful enthusiasm of the German nation, will never forget that within a few days more than a million volunteers entered German barracks to prepare to fight the enemies who were hemming in Germany. Workmen, students, peasants, townspeople, teachers, traders, officials, high and low, all hastened to join the colours. There was such a constant stream of men that finally they had to be sent away, and put off till a later date, for there was neither equipment nor clothing left for them. By 16th August, before the advance in the west had begun, the Prussian War Minister in Berlin had ordered the formation of five new Reserve Corps to be numbered from XXII to XXVI, whilst Bavaria formed the 6th Bavarian Reserve Division, and Saxony and Würtemburg together brought the XXVII Reserve Corps into being. Old and young had taken up arms in August 1914, in their enthusiasm to defend their country, and 75 per cent. of the new Corps consisted of these volunteers, the remainder being trained men of both categories.

The German populace cheering the outbreak of war.

The pickelhaube was the most common form of head-gear at the early part of the war, however it was by no means universal as Jaeger and Landsturm units often sported a different form of hat which, on occasion, led to casualties from friendly fire as the landsturm were similar in style to those of the British and Russians.

A German recruitment rally 1914.

Germany before the Great War was a highly militarized nation. This procession down the Unter Den Linden in 1914 is typical of the military pomp which was at the root cause of the war.

German reservists arrested in Britain.

German infantry on the march.

Germany's air fleet was enhanced by the addition of the Zeppelin airships.

A Zeppelin crew watching another aerial battleship as it proceeds overhead.

The cavalry and the guard regiments were the formations of choice. A career in the artillery was viewed as a less prestigious posting. This is somewhat ironic as it was the artillery which proved to be the most important arm of the army.

His Imperial majesty, Kaiser Wilhelm directs his troops during pre-war manoeuvres.

Shortly after the outbreak of the war, the Kaiser observes an artillery piece being fired in anger.

Officer's rations are issued by the mobile quartermaster's wagon.

A weary band of German prisoners captured by the British at La Ferte.

"Super Huns" the contemporary view of the German leadership as expressed in the pages of *The War Illustrated*.

The whole of German society had been militarized by 1914. Compulsory military service was universal.

A pre-war image of Dragoon Regiment number 25 of the Imperial German Army.

Cavalry of The Imperial German Army on pre-war manoeuvres.

The Imperial German Army in 1914.

CHAPTER 1

THE ROAD TO YPRES

FROM THE PREFACE TO 'THE GERMANS AT YPRES' BY OTTO SCHWINK

There is no more brilliant campaign in history than the advance of our armies against the Western Powers in August and early September 1914. The weak French attacks into Alsace, the short-lived effort to beat back the centre and right wing of our striking-force, the active defence of the Allied hostile armies and the passive resistance of the great Belgian and French fortresses, all failed to stop our triumphal march.

The patriotic devotion and unexampled courage of each individual German soldier, combined with the able leading of his commanders, overcame all opposition and sent home the news of countless German victories. It was not long before the walls and hearts of Paris were trembling, and it seemed as if the conspiracy which half the world had been weaving against us for so many years was to be brought to a rapid conclusion. Then came the Battle of the Marne, in the course of which the centre and right wings of the German Western Army were, it is true, withdrawn, but only to fight again as soon as possible, under more favourable strategic conditions. The enemy, not expecting our withdrawal, only followed slowly, and on 13th September our troops brought him to a standstill along a line extending from the Swiss frontier to the Aisne, north-east of Compiègne. In the trench warfare which now began our pursuers soon discovered that our strength had been by no means broken, or even materially weakened, by the hard fighting.

As early as 5th September, before the Battle of the Marne, the Chief of the German General Staff had ordered the right wing should be reinforced by the newly-formed Seventh Army. It soon became clear to the opposing commanders that any attempt to break through the new German front was doomed to failure, and that a decisive success could only be obtained by making an outflanking movement on a large scale against the German right wing. Thus began what our opponents have called the 'Race to the Sea,' in which each party tried to gain a decision by outflanking the other's western wing.

German army at Brandenburg Gate 1914.

A German cavalry division on manoeuvres.

In Germany soldiers were accompanied, amidst scenes of buoyant optimism, on the journey to the train station by their friends and families. This soldier is accompanied by his wife who shares the burden of his heavy field pack.

The Kaiser's strength of arms soon humbled the subjects of King Albert.

The Great War was the first war to encompass radio communication and the widespread use of the telegram system. Here German engineers are improvising a connection.

The rumbling ammunition wagons in the spectacular procession of the Teutonic War Lord passing down the Boulevard Botanique.

German troops leaving the battle damaged town of Mouland.

German officers eating looted food in a Belgian town. The surface fineries of such a whimsical scene mask the terrible outrages and murders which were actually committed by the German forces.

The Imperial German Army of 1914 was comprised of fit, well trained and enthusiastic men who formed the most powerful army on earth.

German observation ladders.

On the German line of communications. German commissariat wagons passing through the ruined village of Visé with munitions for the main German army in Belgium.

German cavalry raiders crossing the Meuse in a canvas boat.

Men of reserve infantry regiment 208.

Transports of the invading German army in Belgium. Forage wagons passing through Mouland, a village on the Belgian frontier of Holland north of Visé, and one of the first to be burnt by the invading army from Aix la Chapelle.

German troops halting on the way to Brussels. Stopping for the midday ration of bread and ham, served out to them from the field transport.

The flower of the German army in the Brussels Parade. The Kaiser's crack troops were sent to impress the people of Brussels. In this splendid photograph (from a private source in Brussels) a group of Hussar officers is seen in the Chaussée de Louvain studying Belgian papers and enjoying a brief rest before their rush through Belgium to attempt that crushing blow at France which was the keynote of German strategical theory for the first phase of the war.

Germans in the heart of Antwerp as prisoners. The Antwerp populace looked on with feelings of gladness mingled with sorrow as this large draft of German prisoners was marched through their city en route for safe keeping in England.

German troops marching through Brussels.

A mixed column of Germans on the march.

A company of German air scouts receiving telephone instructions from their base.
The air scout service, like the armoured motor-car, constituted a new arm of war. Good work was done by the air scouts on both sides of the firing line, but gradually the superior resource and higher initiative of the British air scout established an individual ascendancy over the German air scout. In his despatch of September 1914, Sir John French wrote regarding the British Flying Corps 'Something in the direction of the mastery of the air has already been established.' (Original 1914 caption from *The War Illustrated*).

This photograph taken shortly after the outbreak of the war shows German cavalrymen near Vise, on their way to attack that town. In the wayside house two men and a woman were captured and shot as spies.

German looters returning to camp. Remorseless in its prosecution of every phase of war by the sternest and most savage measures the German army spared the inhabitants in nothing. Here a party is seen returning from looting a Belgian farmstead. (Original 1914 caption from *The War Illustrated*).

Where innocence is bliss. German troops unloading baggage and ammunition. To the juvenile spectators war is merely an amusing entertainment.

The last stage in the journey to the front is undertaken by narrow gauge railway.

Cattle trucks were utilized for longer journeys and were usually adorned by all manner of jingoistic slogans.

German prisoners under guard are marched into captivity.

German troops in the desolated streets of Liege.

German cavalry camp by the German frontier.

Early war German infantry from an unidentified unit. It is unusual for there to be no distinguishing number on the helmet covers.

Men of the XVth regiment of Uhlans from Schleswig Holstein pose for the camera in Sarrebourg during early August 1914.

German infantry resting in a Belgian farmhouse they have destroyed.

German machine gun company in a Belgian wood. The men are wearing the 1886 pattern shako which was surprisingly common among Imperial Army units particularly the Landwehr.

A German soldier lies dead in an unidentified field in Belgium, August 1914.

German soldiers occupy the Brussels Palais de Justice.

German infantry during the advance into Belgium.

German soldiers performing the spade work which was to become a dreary feature of almost every soldier's life.

The clever repair, by German engineers, of a railway bridge at Tongres.

The Krupp light artillery piece which could be broken down into two mule loads.

The German military commandant of Brussels.

This photograph of German troops wearing Red Cross arm bands but with shouldered rifles and advancing at the march proved to be a propaganda coup for the British.

A rare shot of German troops in action. A hastily erected barricade has been thrown up to protect against a British advance.

German supplies on their way through Belgium to France.

German infantry in the Grande Place, Brussels.

German infantry on the march.

German outpost with soldiers awaiting a Belgian attack.

A Belgian peasant is interrogated by German officers.

German infantry on a train to the frontier. The railway network played a vital role in the planning which led up to the Great War.

Confiscating Belgian cattle to feed the German garrison of Brussels.

A motorized German anti-aircraft gun. These guns were designed to fire at a high angle in order to attack aircraft.

Men of the 2nd regiment of the German Imperial Guards in Brussels.

Officers of the German Imperial Guards in Brussels.

The German field kitchen on the steps of the Palais de Justice, Brussels.

Soldiers of the German Imperial Army in Brussels, 1914.

German troops weary from marching in a Brussels suburb.

A German gun and guards near the Palais de Justice, Brussels.

Field Marshal Von Der Goltz.

The stream of fugitives from Belgium must await processing by the German authorities.

Field kitchen in the murdered Burgomasters garden.

A wounded soldier being cared for by the Belgian Red Cross.

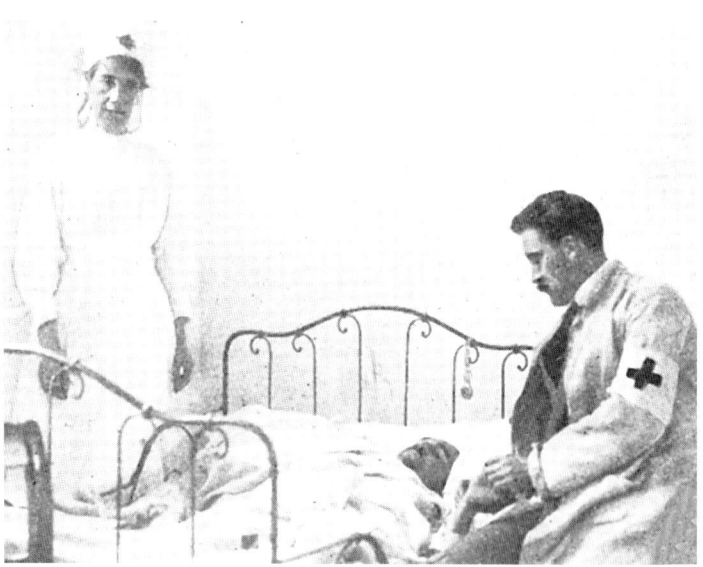

Germans lording it in Belgium.

German invaders doling out a little food to the poor of Bruges.

German Hussars on the attack. The light cavalry provided a screen for the advancing armies.

CHAPTER 2

THE RACE TO THE SEA

FROM THE PREFACE TO 'THE GERMANS AT YPRES'
BY OTTO SCHWINK

The good communications of France, especially in the north, enabled the Allied troops to be moved far more rapidly than our own, for the German General Staff had at their disposal only the few Franco-Belgian railways which had been repaired, and these were already overburdened with transport of material of every description. In spite of this, however, the French and British attacks failed to drive back the German right wing at any point. Not only did they find German troops ready to meet them in every case, but we were also generally able to keep the initiative in our hands.

In this manner by the end of September the opposing flanks had been extended to the district north of the Somme, about Péronne-Albert. A few days later began the interminable fighting round Arras and Lens, and by the middle of October our advanced troops were near Lille, marching through the richest industrial country of France. The Army Cavalry was placed so as to threaten the hostile left flank, and to bring pressure against the communications with England. Our cavalry patrols pushed forward as far as Cassel and Hazebrouck, the pivots of the enemy's movements, but they had to retire eastwards again when superior hostile forces moved up to the north-east. The reports which they brought back with them all pointed to preparations by the enemy for an attack on a large scale, and for another effort to turn the fortunes of the campaign to his favour. With this in view all available troops, including newly-arrived detachments from England, were to be used to break through the gap between Lille and Antwerp against our right wing, roll it up and begin the advance against the northern Rhine.

It must be remembered that at the time this plan was conceived the fortresses of Lille and Antwerp were still in French and Belgian possession. It was hoped that Lille, with its well-built fortifications, even though they were not quite up-to-date, would at least hold up the German right wing for a time. Antwerp was defended by the whole Belgian Army of from five to six divisions which were to be reinforced by British troops, and it was confidently expected that this garrison would be sufficiently strong to hold the most modern fortress in Western Europe against any attack, especially if, as was generally believed, this could only be carried out by comparatively weak forces. Thus it seemed that the area of concentration for the Franco-Belgian masses was secure until all preparations were ready for the blow to be delivered through weakly-held Belgium against the rear of the German armies in the west. The plan was a bold one, but it was countered by a big attack of considerable German forces in the same neighbourhood and at the same time. The two opponents met and held each other up on the Yser and at Ypres, and here the last hope of our enemy to seize Belgium and gain possession of the rich provinces of Northern France before the end of the year was frustrated. The question arises how the Germans were able to find the men to do this, since it had been necessary to send considerable forces to the Eastern front to stop the Russian advance.

The famous German Uhlans advancing at the gallop.

German pioneers on the march.

German troops moving towards the Belgian frontier are presented with flowers by an excited population.

The famous image of German infantry on the advance in 1914.

German trenches on the Aisne. These rudimentary constructions were the forerunners of a system which eventually stretched from Belgium to Switzerland.

The Imperial German Army advancing Flanders, August 1914.

German troops on the advance during 1914 in the short period before the advent of trench warfare.

The German invaders watering their horses in a fast moving stream.

Germans shelter under haystacks at Mons and Charleroi.

After hours of tortuous thirst on the battlefield the advancing troops are finally able to obtain some much needed water.

The German Empress presenting roses to Guards officers.

A German spy meeting his death by firing squad.

Franc-tireurs, irregular combatants who carry arms but do not wear uniforms. The Germans did not recognize them as soldiers and treated them as non-combatants caught with arms. During the war hundreds, if not thousands, were led out to be shot.

German dead on the morning after the Battle of Langemarck which became known as the *Kindermort* or 'slaughter of the innocents'.

CHAPTER 3

LILLE, ANTWERP AND BEYOND

FROM THE PREFACE TO 'THE GERMANS AT YPRES' BY OTTO SCHWINK

The transport of the XXII, XXIII, XXIV, XXVI and XXVII Reserve Corps to the Western Front began on 10th October, and the 6th Bavarian Reserve Division followed shortly after. Only comparatively few experienced commanders were available for the units, and it was left to their keen and patriotic spirit to compensate as far as possible for what the men still lacked to play their part in the great struggle.

The situation of the armies on the Western Front at this time was as follows. In the neighbourhood of Lille the northern wing of the Sixth Army was fighting against an ever-increasing enemy. On 9th October, Antwerp, in spite of its strong fortifications and garrison, was taken after a twelve days' siege directed by General von Beseler, commanding the III Reserve Corps, and well known in peace time as Chief of the Engineer Corps and Inspector-General of Fortifications. The victorious besiegers had carried all before them. As they were numerically insufficient to invest Antwerp on the west, south and east, a break-through was attempted on a comparatively narrow front. It was completely successful, and Antwerp was occupied; but the main body of the Belgian army, in good fighting order, was able to escape westwards along the coast, to await the arrival of British and French reinforcements behind the Yser. Only about 5,000 Belgians were taken prisoner, but some 20,000 Belgian and 2,000 British troops were forced into Holland. In consequence of this new situation, and of the reports of hostile concentrations in the area Calais-Dunkirk-Lille, the German General Staff decided to form a new Fourth Army under Duke Albert of Würtemburg. It was to be composed of the XXII, XXIII, XXVI, and XXVII Reserve Corps, and was joined later on by the III Reserve Corps with the 4th Ersatz Division. By 13th October the detainment of this new Army was in full progress west and south-west of Brussels. On the evening of 14th October the four Reserve Corps began their march to the line Eecloo (fifteen miles east of Bruges) – Deynze – point four miles west of Audenarde.

In the meantime we had occupied the fortified town of Lille. It had been entered on 12th October by part of the XIX Saxon Corps and some Landwehr troops, after the town had suffered considerably owing to the useless efforts of French territorial troops to defend it. The order to the garrison was: 'The town is to be held till the Tenth French Army arrives'; it resulted in the capture of 4,500 French prisoners, who were sent to Germany. On the 14th the right wing of the Sixth Army, consisting of the XIII Würtemburg and XIX Saxon Corps, pushed forward to the Lys, behind a screen of three Cavalry Corps. They took up a position covering Lille, from Menin through Comines to Warneton and thence east of Armentières, where they came into touch with the 14th Infantry Division which was further south near the western forts of Lille. To the north of the Sixth Army, the III Reserve Corps, with its three divisions from Antwerp, was advancing westwards on a broad front. By the 14th it had driven back the hostile rear guards and reached a line from Bruges to near Ghent. Airmen and reconnaissance detachments had recognized movements of large bodies of troops about Hazebrouck, Lillers and St. Omer and reported disembarkations on a big scale at Dunkirk and Calais. In addition to this, considerable hostile forces had reached Ypres, and appeared to be facing more or less southwards opposite the northern wing of the Sixth Army.

An order issued on 14th October, by the Chief of the German General Staff, gave the following instructions for the German forces between Lille and the sea. The Sixth Army was at first to remain entirely on the defensive along the line Menin-Armentières-La Bassée and to await the attack of our new Fourth Army against the left flank of the enemy. The offensive action of the Fourth Army after its deployment was to be so directed that the III Reserve Corps, which now belonged to it, should move as its right wing in echelon along the coast, whilst its left was to advance through Menin.

In accordance with these orders the III Reserve Corps occupied Ostend on the 15th, its left wing reaching the line of the Thourout–Roulers road. The Corps was then ordered not to advance further for a few days, so as to avoid the attention of the British and French, who were advancing against the north wing of the Sixth Army, being drawn prematurely to movements in this neighbourhood. Only patrols therefore were sent out to reconnoitre across the Yser and the canal south of it. On the 17th the XXII, XXIII, XXVI and XXVII Reserve Corps reached the line Oostcamp (south of Bruges)-Thielt--point six miles east of Courtrai. On the advance of these four new Corps, the III Reserve Corps was to draw away to the right wing, and during the 17th and the following morning it moved up to the sector of attack allotted to it immediately south of the coast, and cleared the front of the Fourth Army. The reconnaissance activity of the previous days had in places led to severe fighting, especially on the southern wing in front of the 6th Reserve Division. It was found that the Belgian rearguards still held part of the ground east of the Yser and of the canal to Ypres. Any attempt to advance beyond this water-barrier was out of the question, as the bridges had been blown up and the whole line put in a state of defence.

The screening of the advancing Fourth Army by the III Reserve Corps was a brilliant success. At midday on the 18th, Field-Marshal French, who was to direct the enemy's attack from the line of the Yser, was still in ignorance of our new Army. He believed he had time to prepare for his attack, and his only immediate care was to secure the line from Armentières to the sea for the deployment. After the events on the Marne, Field-Marshal French had particularly requested General Joffre, the Allied commander, that he might be placed on the northern flank of the line. He would then be close to Calais, which had already become an English town, he would be able to protect the communications to his country; and, further, the fame to be gained by a decisive and final victory attracted this ambitious commander to the north. As a result the II British Corps under General Smith-Dorrien was now in action against the strong German positions between Vermelles (four miles south-west of La Bassée) and Laventie (west of Lille). Further to the north the III British Corps was fighting against the Saxons advancing from Lille and our I, II and IV Cavalry Corps. The I British Cavalry Corps was covering the hostile advance on the line Messines–Gheluvelt, south-east of Ypres. Immediately to the north again, the newly formed IV British Corps, consisting of the 7th Infantry Division and 3rd Cavalry Division, had arrived in the area Gheluvelt–Zonnebeke, pursued in its retreat by von Beseler's columns (III Reserve Corps). On its left the I British Corps had marched up to Bixschoote, and the gap between this place and Dixmude had been closed by a French Cavalry Division which connected up with the Belgian Army. The last, reinforced by two French Territorial divisions, was engaged in preparing the line of the Yser up to the sea for the most stubborn defence. These strong forces were to cover the arrival of the VIII and X French Corps and were to deliver the first blow against our supposed right wing.

On the 18th one of our cyclist patrols which had gone out far in advance of its Corps was surrounded near Roulers, and it was only by its capture that the enemy definitely discovered the arrival of the new German Corps, whose formation, however, had not been unknown to him, thanks to his good Secret Service system. Field-Marshal French was now confronted with a new situation. The preparations for his big attack were not yet completed. The superiority of the masses already concentrated did not yet appear to him to be sufficient to guarantee success against the enemy's advance. The British commander therefore decided to remain on the defensive against our new Fourth Army, until the completion of the French concentration. His line was already closed up to the sea, it was naturally strong, and fresh troops were arriving daily. The danger threatening Dunkirk and Calais had the effect of making England put forth her full energy; the British troops fought desperately to defend every inch of ground, using every possible means to keep up the sinking spirits of the Belgians. They demanded and received rapid assistance from the French, and were backed up by fresh reinforcements from England.

German troops resting in a sunken road.

German infantry take up defensive positions 1914.

German troops marching through Belgium 1914.

German troops in full kit crossing open fields during the invasion of Western Europe 1914.

The Kaiser and Moltke.

The Kaiser and Ruprecht.

Cheerful German infantrymen on the march into Belgium.

German troops at rest in Belgium 1914.

Light German cavalry conducting a reconnaissance These mounted troops provide a screen in front of the advancing armies.

The men of Landwehr Infantry Regiment No. 1.

British and German dead lying side by side after hand to hand combat in Langemarck.

German officers observing the fall of artillery fire.

The German advance continues.

British prisoners with their German guards. These men faced four desolate and brutal years in captivity.

The German army was not above using the Red Cross as cover. Here ammunition was being transported in a rail carriage marked with the Red Cross.

In order to counter the successful Allied propaganda campaign which depicted the Germans as barbarians this photograph of German soldiers enjoying cordial relations with the civilian population was widely circulated.

English trenches destroyed by German artillery near Armentiéres.

Kaiser consults a map.

A field kitchen slaughtering its own ingredients under the hungry gaze of would be diners.

A German military band leads a church parade.

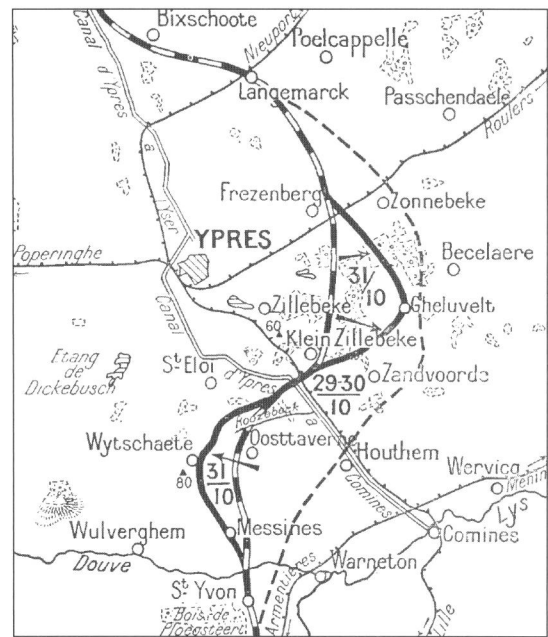

The Ypres salient 31st October 1914.

A good study of a Bavarian rifleman in full marching order.

Lightly wounded German cavalrymen have their wounds tended in the aftermath of a skirmish outside Liege.

An excellent study of an early German trench. As the power of artillery grew simple structures such as this were proved woefully inadequate.

German limbers and ammunition lie discarded on the battlefield following the German retreat from the Marne.

German field artillery in action.

A German field gun crew.

Opposite: The German officer corps was the preserve of the nobility and the upper class, but they still found time for high jinks in front of the camera.

The beginnings of trench warfare. Here Belgian prisoners are forced to dig trenches to be occupied by their German captors. In a remarkably short time this network would soon extend from the Belgian coast all the way to the Swiss border.

A German soldier draws a caricature of General Joffre on the wagon of a troop train. The artist has captioned his work 'Express to Paris.'

German soldiers dine alfresco at children's benches removed from a Belgian schoolhouse.

Opposite: The warriors of 1914 pose for the camera.

This photograph, which was taken prior to the 1914 Christmas truce, features German soldiers resting in their trench in the snow.

German jaegers taking up firing positions under a bridge destroyed by the retreating Belgian army.

German staff officers being driven in an unusual three wheeled transport.

German troops, on September 1st, marching Into Amiens, the famous French city of about 100,000 Inhabitants which was later destined to become a key British supply centre.

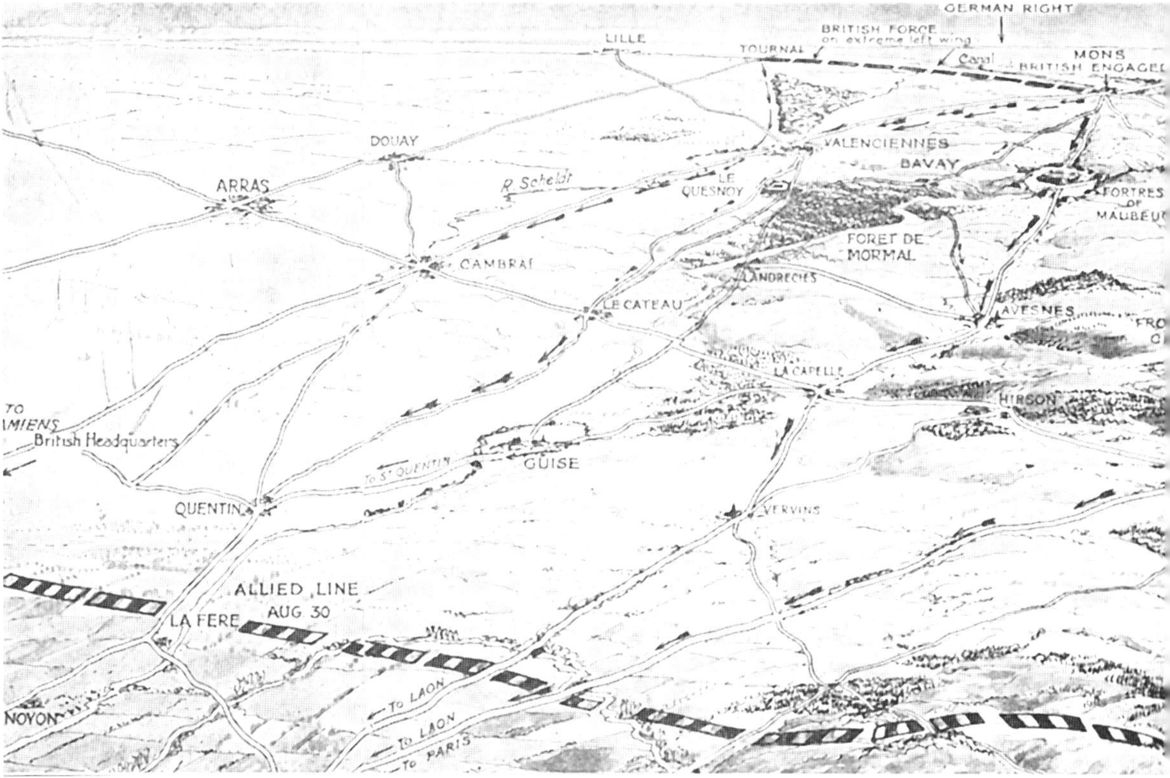

The British held the left wing as the French army fell back from the Sambre to the Amiens-Laon line.

Improvised stables for some of the millions of horses which provided the power to transport the German armies.

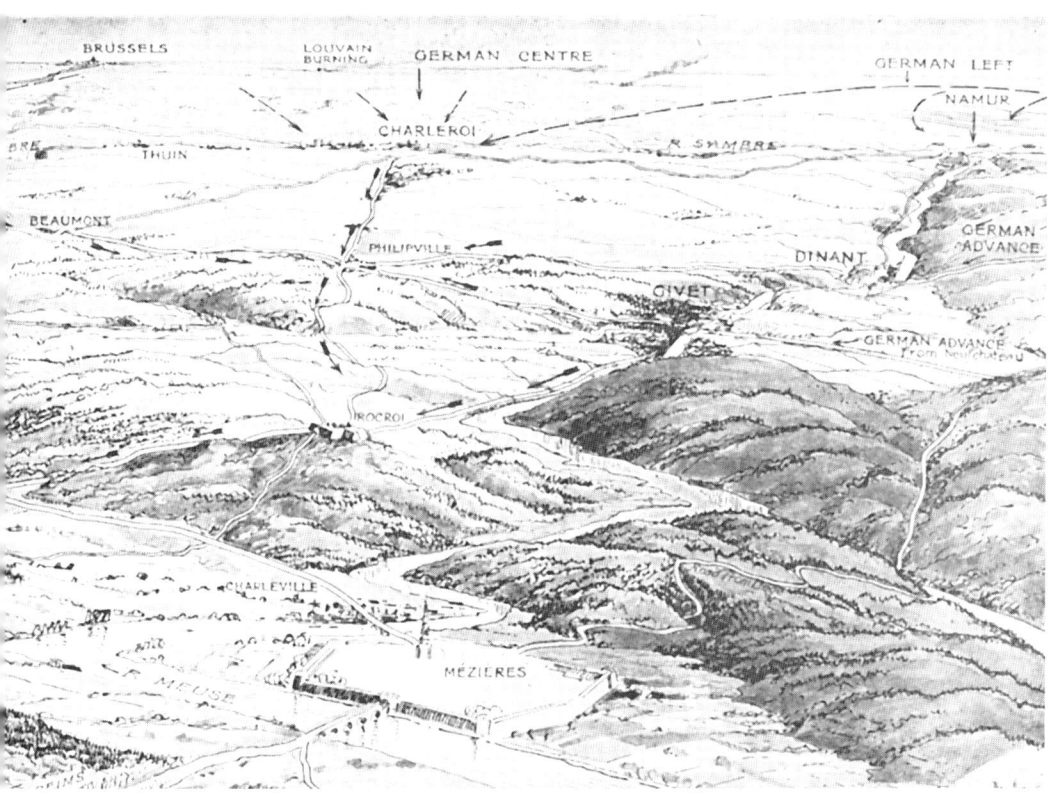

German troops settle down in their crowded billet.

CHAPTER 4
THE FIRST BATTLE OF YPRES

FROM THE PREFACE TO 'THE GERMANS AT YPRES'
BY OTTO SCHWINK

From the German point of view the patriotic enthusiasm and unconditional determination to win the war which pervaded the new Fourth Army gave every prospect of successfully closing with the enemy, who was apparently still engaged in concentrating and reorganizing his forces, and gaining Calais, the aim and object of the 1914 campaign.

Our offensive, however, struck against a powerful army, fully deployed and ready to meet us. The British boast that they held up our attack with a great inferiority of numbers, but this was only true in the case of the 7th Division during the first two days in the small sector Zonnebeke–Gheluvelt. On 22nd October between Armentières and the sea there were eight Corps opposed to the seven attacking German Corps; and, besides, the enemy had prepared a series of lines of strong trenches covered by an extensive system of artificial obstacles. In the course of the operations that developed, the relative strength of the opposing forces never appreciably altered in our favour. The moral strength of our troops made up for the numerical superiority of the enemy. Our attack drove the hostile lines well back and destroyed, it is hoped for ever, the ambition of our opponent to regain Belgium by force of arms.

The great desire of the Germans to defeat the hostile northern wing, and to hit hardest the most hated of all our enemies, and, on the other side, the obstinate determination of the British to hold on to the passages to their country, and to carry out the offensive to the Rhine with all their resources, resulted in this battle being one of the most severe of the whole war. The deeds of our troops, old and young, in the battle on the Yser and of Ypres can never be sufficiently praised, and in spite of great losses their enthusiasm remained unchecked and their offensive spirit unbroken.

A lightly wounded German soldier pictured during the fighting at Ypres.

German artillery on the move 1914.

The 7.7cm German field gun was the standard equipment for field batteries during the war.

German infantry moving forward in a relatively cautious manner by digging in as they advance.

German gunners in front of their well screened artillery piece consider the next target.

Prussian infantry wearing linen trouser-overalls, fastened by the two bands over the shoulders, line up for inspection. The workings of the rifles are bandaged to prevent them becoming clogged with mud from the trenches.

German officers studying their maps in order to plot the next move during the advance .

CHAPTER 5
THE CHRISTMAS TRUCE

Although there was no official truce, roughly 100,000 British and German troops were involved in a spontaneous and unofficial cessation of fighting along the length of the Western Front. The first truce started on Christmas Eve, 24th December 1914, when German troops began decorating their trenches in the area around Ypres and Ploegsteert.

The Germans began by placing candles on their trenches and on Christmas trees, then continued the celebration by singing Christmas carols. The British responded by singing carols of their own. The two sides then continued by shouting Christmas greetings to each other. Soon thereafter, there were excursions across no man's land, where small gifts were exchanged, such as food, tobacco and alcohol, and souvenirs such as buttons and hats. The artillery in the region fell silent. The truce also allowed a breathing spell where recently killed soldiers could be brought back behind their lines by burial parties. Joint services were also held. In many sectors, the truce lasted through Christmas night, but it continued until New Year's Day in others.

The cartoonist Bruce Bairnsfather, was present at the truce and he recorded the events for posterity: 'I wouldn't have missed that unique and weird Christmas Day for anything. ... I spotted a German officer, some sort of lieutenant I should think, and being a bit of a collector, I intimated to him that I had taken a fancy to some of his buttons. ... I brought out my wire clippers and, with a few deft snips, removed a couple of his buttons and put them in my pocket. I then gave him two of mine in exchange. ... The last I saw was one of my machine gunners, who was a bit of an amateur hairdresser in civil life, cutting the unnaturally long hair of a docile Boche, who was patiently kneeling on the ground whilst the automatic clippers crept up the back of his neck.'

A letter written by a doctor attached to the Rifle Brigade, published in *The Times* on 1 January 1915, reported 'a football match... played between them and us in front of the trench.' Royal Field Artillery Lieutenant Albert Wynn wrote of a match against a German team (described as 'Prussians and Hanovers') played near Ypres. Games are certainly reported to have been played between teams of opposing armies and include that of the '133rd Royal Saxon Regiment who played a game against "Scottish troops"'. Another match was played in the sector of Argyll and Sutherland Highlanders in a letter home published by the *Glasgow News* on 2 January, it was recorded that a game was played in his sector 'between the lines and the trenches,' and, according to the letter, "the Scots" won by a margin of 4–1.

Opposite: One of a number of photographs which was taken in no man's land during the Christmas truce of 1914 features both British and German soldiers.

British and German troops hold a temporary truce in 1914.

Men of both sides pose for a photograph during the Christmas truce 1914.

Opposite: German troops, obviously some way from the front, celebrating New Year's Eve

German comrades celebrating during the festive season 1914-1915.

British and German officers fraternizing near Ypres, December 1914.

German cyclists were widely deployed on the advance into Belgium and France.

A gun carriage under repair in a German mobile workshop behind the front.

German howitzers prepare to bombard the British positions in the salient.

German troops involved in a spirited 1914 Christmas celebration.

CHAPTER 6

THE THEATRE OF OPERATIONS

FROM THE PREFACE TO 'THE GERMANS AT YPRES'
BY OTTO SCHWINK

The country in which it was hoped to bring about the final decision of the campaign of 1914 was not favourable to an attack from east to west.

Western Flanders, the most western part of Belgium, is almost completely flat, and lies only slightly above sea-level, and in some parts is even below it. Mount Kemmel, in the south, is the only exception; rising to a height of over 500 feet, it is the watch-tower of Western Flanders. Before the war it was a well-wooded ridge with pretty enclosures and villages. From its slopes and summits could be seen the whole countryside from Lille to Menin and Dixmude.

The possession of this hill was of great importance. Our cavalry actually occupied it during the early days of October, but when the enemy advanced he immediately attacked it. The XIX Saxon Corps was still too far away to help, and so Mount Kemmel fell into the enemy's hands. During the battle of Ypres it was his best observation post, and of the utmost assistance to his artillery.

We repeatedly succeeded in gaining a footing on the eastern crest of the ridge in front of Ypres, but in the autumn of 1914, as also later in the war, this was always the signal for the most desperate fighting. It was thus that the heights of St Eloi, the high-lying buildings of Hooge and the village of Wytschaete won their sanguinary fame.

Lying in the midst of luxuriant meadows, with its high ramparts and fine buildings, Ypres was formerly one of the most picturesque towns in Flanders. In the fourteenth century it had a considerable importance, and became the centre of the cloth-weaving trade on its introduction from Italy. Bruges, lying close to the coast, became the market for its wares. The Clothweavers' Guild, which accumulated great wealth, erected in Ypres a fine Gothic hall, whose towers with those of St Martin's Church were landmarks for miles round. In modern times, however, the importance of the town greatly diminished. The cloth-weaving industry drifted away to the factories of Menin and Courtrai; and Ypres, like its dead neighbour Bruges, remained only a half-forgotten memory of its former brilliance.

The war has brought fresh importance to the town, but of a mournful kind. On the impact of the German and Anglo-French masses in Flanders in the autumn of 1914, it became the central pivot of the operations. The enemy dug his heels into the high ground in front of it; for, as an Englishman has written, it had become a point of honour to hold the town. Ypres lay so close to the front that our advance could be seen from its towers, and the enemy was able to use it for concealing his batteries and sheltering his reserves. For the sake of our troops we had to bring it under fire; for German life is more precious than the finest Gothic architecture. Thus the mythical death of Ypres became a reality: no tower now sends forth its light across the countryside, and a wilderness of wrecked and burnt-out houses replaces the pretty town so full of legend and tradition in the history of Flanders.

The streams which run northwards from the hills about Ypres unite for the most part near the town and flow into the Yser canal, which connects the Lys at Comines with the sea at Nieuport. This canal passes through the Ypres ridge near Hollebeke and, following northwards the course of a small canalized tributary of the Yser, meets the Yser itself south of Dixmude. The dunes at Nieuport have been cut through by engineers for its exit to the sea. It is only from Dixmude northwards that the canal becomes an obstacle which requires proper bridging equipment for its passage. Its high embankments to the south of Dixmude, however, give excellent cover in the otherwise flat country and greatly simplify the task of the defender.

The canal acquired a decisive importance when the hard-pressed Belgians, during the battle on the night of 29th–30th October, let in the sea at flood-tide through the sluices into the canal, and then by blowing up the sluice-gates at Nieuport, allowed it to flood the battlefield along the lower Yser. By this means they succeeded in placing broad stretches of country under water, so much so that any extensive military operations in that district became out of the question. The high water-level greatly influenced all movements over a very large area. By his order the King of the Belgians destroyed for years the natural wealth of a considerable part of his fertile country, for the sea-water must have ruined all vegetation down to its very roots.

The country on both sides of the canal is flat, and difficult for observation purposes. The high level of the water necessitates drainage of the meadows, which for this purpose are intersected by deep dykes which have muddy bottoms. The banks of the dykes are bordered with willows, and thick-set hedges form the boundaries of the cultivated areas. Generally speaking, the villages do not consist of groups of houses: the farms are dispersed either singly, or in rows forming a single street. The country is densely populated and is consequently well provided with roads. But these are only good where they have been made on embankments and are paved. The frequent rains, which begin towards the end of October, rapidly turn the other roads into mere mud tracks and in many cases make them quite useless for long columns of traffic.

The digging of trenches was greatly complicated by rain and surface-water. The loam soil was on the whole easy to work in; but it was only on the high ground that trenches could be dug deep enough to give sufficient cover against the enemy's artillery fire; on the flat, low-lying ground they could not in many cases be made more than two feet deep.

A few miles south of the coast the country assumes quite another character: there are no more hedges and canals: instead gently rolling sand-hills separate the land from the sea, and this deposited sand is not fertile like the plains south of them. A belt of dunes prevents the sea encroaching on the land.

The greatest trouble of the attacker in all parts of Flanders is the difficulty of observation. The enemy, fighting in his own country, had every advantage, while our artillery observation posts were only found with the utmost trouble. Our fire had to be directed from the front line, and it frequently happened that our brave artillerymen had to bring up their guns into the front infantry lines in order to use them effectively. Although the enemy was able to range extremely accurately on our guns which were thus quickly disclosed, nothing could prevent the German gunners from following the attacking infantry.

Observation from aeroplanes was made very difficult by the many hedges and villages, so that it took a long time to discover the enemy's dispositions and give our artillery good targets.

Finally, the flat nature of the country and the consequent limitations of view were all to the advantage of the defenders, who were everywhere able to surprise the attackers. Our troops were always finding fresh defensive lines in front of them without knowing whether they were occupied or not. The British, many of whom had fought in a colonial war against the most cunning of enemies in equally difficult country, allowed the attacker to come to close quarters and then opened a devastating fire at point-blank range from rifles and machine-guns concealed in houses and trees.

In many cases the hedges and dykes split up the German attacks so that even the biggest operations degenerated into disconnected actions which made the greatest demands on the powers of endurance and individual skill of our volunteers. In spite of all these difficulties our men, both old and young, even when left to act on their own initiative, showed a spirit of heroism and self-sacrifice which makes the battle on the Yser a sacred memory both for the Army and the Nation, and every one who took part in it may say with pride, 'I was there.'

A contemporary view of the Ypres salient.

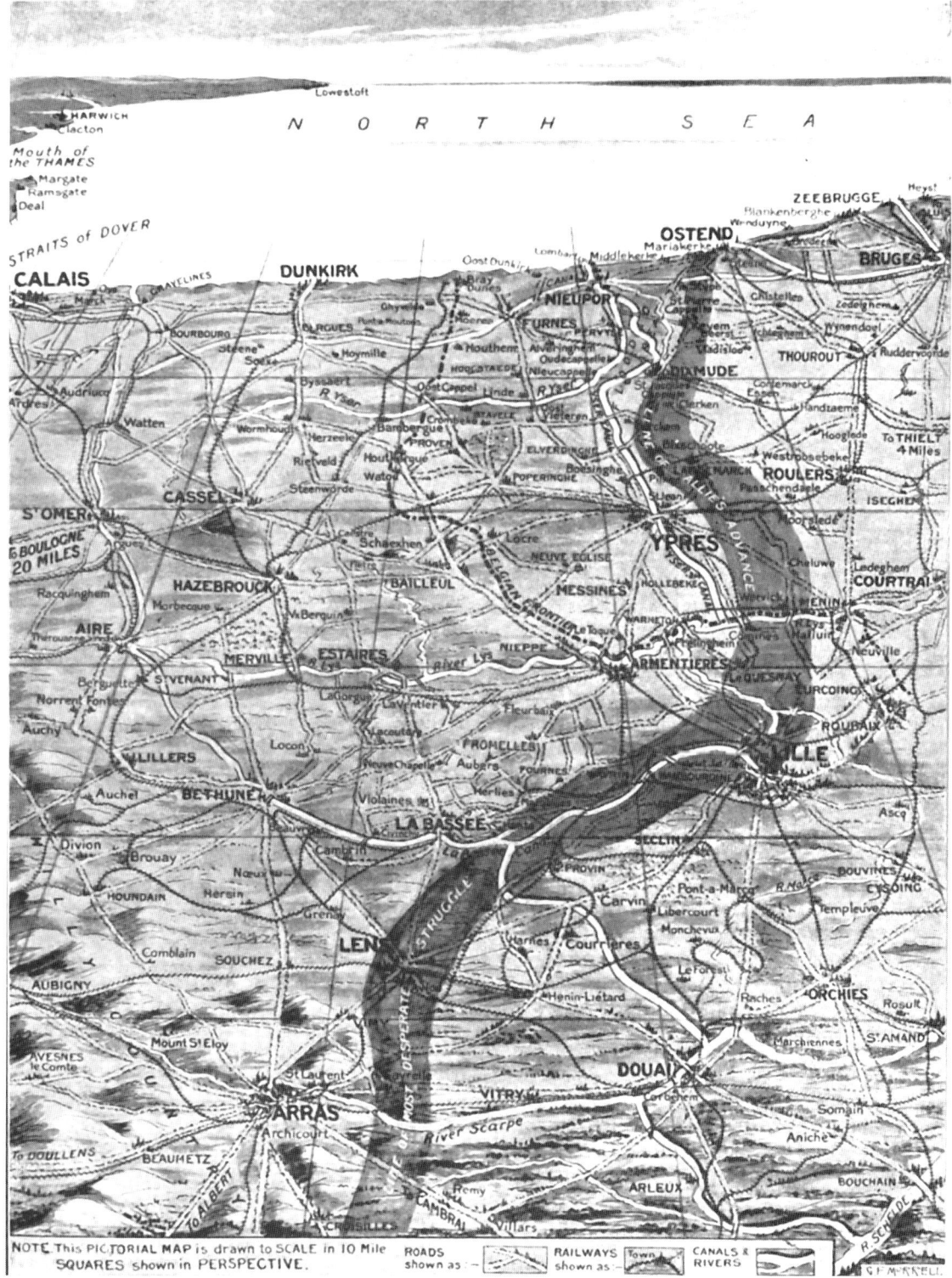

German soldiers display rats killed in their trench. The German soldier was less fastidious than his British counterparts, and many rats were in fact eaten.

This well maintained German trench from 1916 demonstrates the thoroughness with which the German lines were constructed once the lines surrounding the salient had become established.

German troops at ease in a third line trench.

The huge number of horses which the German army required had to be specially housed and cared for during the unexpectedly harsh winter of 1914.

Opposite: The well constructed German trenches proved a formidable barrier in 1915. British artillery, although increasing in strength, had not yet reached the overwhelming power and potency which would reduce the German lines of defence to a series of connected shell holes.

The German women were not going to be defeated by the difficulties of keeping a pickelhaube wearer warm in the winter of 1914.

Freezing Bavarian artillerymen on the perimeter of the Ypres salient in the winter of 1914.

German troops on the beach at Ostend .

Opposite: As soon as trench warfare became established the problem of lice became apparent.

A German trench in the Ypres salient.

Photographed behind the German lines, a well screened howitzer bombards the british positions.

For German soldiers de-lousing became a regular ritual in a battle which could never be won.

A German outpost in Belgium lies under a blanket of snow during the winter of 1914.

Mail is delivered to shivering soldiers taking cover in a shell hole.

Above and below: German infantry set to work on a carpentry task. The German skill in working with wood was often demonstrated in their trench systems.

CHAPTER 7

THE BRITISH RESPONSE

FROM THE INTRODUCTION TO THE 1919 ENGLISH TRANSLATION OF 'THE GERMANS AT YPRES'
BY OTTO SCHWINK

Field-Marshal Viscount Francis, in his book *1914*, has said that the period 27th to 31st October during the first Battle of Ypres was 'more momentous and fateful than any other which I directed during my period of service as Commander-in-Chief in the field. 31st October and 1st November will remain for ever memorable in the history of our country, for during those two days no more than a thin and straggling line of tired-out British soldiers stood between the Empire and its practical ruin as an independent first-class Power.'

The German account accentuates the truth of Lord French's appreciation of the great peril in which the Army and the Nation stood. It tells us of the enemy's plans, and of the large forces that he brought up with great skill and secrecy to carry them out, and, generally, to use Marshal Foch's expression, lets us 'know what was going on in the other fellow's house'. But it does more than that: unconsciously perhaps, it bears convincing testimony to the fighting powers of the British Army, the determination of its leaders, the extraordinary effectiveness of the fire of its artillery and of its cavalry and infantry, and the skill of its engineers; for it repeatedly credits Field-Marshal Sir John French with 'reinforcements in abundance,' insists that our troops 'fought desperately for every heap of stones and every pile of bricks before abandoning them,' and definitely records that 'the fact that neither the enemy's commanders nor their troops gave way under the strong pressure we put on them ... gives us the opportunity to acknowledge that there were men of real worth opposed to us who did their duty thoroughly.' We are further told that the effect of our artillery was such that 'it was not possible to push up reserves owing to heavy artillery fire'; that 'all roads leading to the rear were continuously shelled for a long way back'; that the German 'advancing columns were under accurate artillery fire at long range'; that our shells 'blocked streets and bridges and devastated villages so far back that any regular transport of supplies became impossible.' As regards rifle and machine-gun fire, we are credited with 'quantities of machine-guns,' 'large numbers of machine-guns,' etc; with the result that 'the roads were swept by machine-guns'; and that 'over every bush, hedge and fragment of wall floated a thin film of smoke betraying a machine-gun rattling out bullets.' At that date we had no machine-gun units, and there were only two machine-guns on the establishment of a battalion, and of these many had been damaged, and had not yet been replaced; actually machine-guns were few and far between. The only inference to be drawn is that the rapid fire of the British rifleman, were he infantryman, cavalryman or sapper, was mistaken for machine-gun fire both as regards volume and effect. Our simple defences, to complete which both time and labour had been lacking, became in German eyes 'a well-planned maze of trenches,' 'a maze of obstacles and entrenchments'; and we had 'turned every house, every wood and every wall into a strong point'; 'the villages of Wytschaete and Messines had been converted into fortresses' (Festungen); as also the edge of a wood near Gheluvelt and Langemarck. As at the last-named place there was only a small redoubt with a garrison of two platoons, and the 'broad wire entanglements' described by the German General Staff were in reality but trifling obstacles of the kind that the Germans 'took in their stride,'[1] the lavish praise, were it not for the result of the battle, might be deemed exaggerated. Part of it undoubtedly is. It is fair, however, to deduce that the German nation had to be given some explanation why the 'contemptible little Army' had not been pushed straightway into the sea.

The monograph is frankly intended to present the views that the German General Staff wish should be held as regards the battles, and prevent, as their Preface says, the currency of 'the legends and rumours which take such an easy hold on the popular imagination and are so difficult, if not impossible, to correct afterwards.' One cannot naturally expect the whole truth to be revealed yet; that it is not will be seen from the notes. The elder von Moltke said, when pressed by his nephews to write a true account of 1870–1 – to their future financial advantage. It can't be done yet. Too many highly placed personages (Hohe Herrschaften) would suffer in their reputations.' It was not until twenty-five years after the Franco-Prussian War that Fritz Hönig, Kunz and other German military historians who had been given access to the records, were allowed to draw back the veil a little. The publication of the French General Staff account began even later. What is now given to us is, however, amply sufficient to follow the main German plans and movements; but the difficulties that prevented the enemy from making successful use of the enormous number of troops at his disposal and his superior equipment in heavy artillery, machine-guns, aeroplanes, hand-grenades and other trench warfare material, are untold. Until we learn more we may fairly attribute our victory to the military qualities of the British, French and Belgian troops, and the obstinate refusal of all ranks to admit defeat.

The German General Staff specially claim that the first Battle of Ypres was a German victory, 'for it marked the failure of the enemy's intention to fall on the rear of our Western Armies, to free the rich districts of Northern France and the whole of Belgium,' etc etc. Granted that we did so fail, the battle can, on that General Staff's own evidence, be regarded as a drawn one. For it is definitely stated in the monograph that the object of the operations was 'successfully closing with the enemy ... and gaining CALAIS, the aim and object of the 1914 campaign – this the German Army notoriously did not do. The intention to break through is repeatedly stated: 'although fresh reinforcements had been sent up by the German General Staff ... a break-through had not been possible.' 'Another effort to break through should be made as soon as possible.' We are told that Fabeck's Army Group (eventually nine infantry and five cavalry divisions) was formed 'as a strong new army of attack for breaking through on the front Werwicq–Warneton.' Linsingen's

Army Group (five divisions) after the failure of von Fabeck was formed 'to drive back and crush the enemy lying north of the (Comines–Ypres) canal ... and to break through there.' Finally, however, it is admitted that 'no break-through of the enemy's lines had been accomplished.... We had not succeeded in making the decisive break-through, and the dream of ending the campaign in the west in our favour had to be consigned to its grave.' In fact, the book is largely an apologia and a confession of failure which mere protestations of victory cannot alter.

The effects of a German victory on the course of the war, with the Channel ports in German hands, as compared with those of an Allied victory in Flanders, which at that period of the war and at that season of the year could have resulted in little more than pushing the enemy back into Belgium a few miles, may be easily imagined. If the battle was a tactical draw, at least we had a strategic balance in our favour.

The principal reasons advanced for the German ill-success are 'the enemy's numerical superiority, and the strength of his positions,' and of course the drastic course taken by the Belgians of 'calling in the sea to their aid'.

There is constant repetition of these pleas throughout the book. To those who were there and saw our 'thin and straggling line' and the hastily constructed and lightly wired defences: mere isolated posts and broken lengths of shallow holes with occasional thin belts of wire, and none of the communication trenches of a later date, they provoke only amazement. Even German myopia cannot be the cause of such statements.

As regards the superiority of numbers, the following appears to be the approximate state of the case as regards the infantry on the battle front from Armentières (inclusive) to the sea dealt with in the monograph. It is necessary to count in battalions, as the Germans had two or three with each cavalry division, and the British Commander-in-Chief enumerates the reinforcements sent up to Ypres from the II and Indian Corps by battalions, and two Territorial battalions, London Scottish and Hertfordshires, also took part. The total figures are: British, French, Belgian 263 battalions, German 426 battalions.

That is roughly a proportion of Allies to Germans of 13 to 21. Viscount French in his *1914* says 7 to 12 Corps, which is much the same: 52 to 84 as against 49 to 84, and very different from the German claim of '40 divisions to 25'. Actually in infantry divisions the Allies had only 22, even counting as complete the Belgian six, which had only the strength of German brigades. Any future correction of the figures, when actual bayonets present can be counted, will probably emphasize the German superiority in numbers still more, and the enemy indisputably had the advantage of united command, homogeneous formations and uniform material which were lacking in the Allied force.

As regards the cavalry the Western Allies had six divisions, including one of three brigades. The enemy had at least nine, possibly more (one, the Guard Cavalry Division, of three brigades), as it is not clear from the German account how much cavalry was transferred from the Sixth Army to the Fourth Army.[2] It may be noted that a German cavalry division included, with its two or three cavalry brigades, horse artillery batteries and the two or three Jäger battalions, three or more machine-gun batteries and two or more companies of cyclists; and was thus, unlike ours, a force of all arms.

The German General Staff reveal nothing about the exact strength of the artillery. In a footnote it is mentioned that in addition to infantry divisions the III Reserve Corps contained siege artillery, Pionier formations and other technical troops; and in the text that 'all the available heavy artillery of the Sixth Army to be brought up (to assist the

Fourth Army) for the break-through.' The Germans had trench-mortars (*Minenwerfer*) which are several times mentioned, whilst our first ones were still in the process of improvisation by the Engineers of the Indian Corps at Bethune.

The statement that 'the enemy's' (i.e. British, French and Belgian) 'superiority in material, in guns, trench-mortars, machine-guns and aeroplanes, etc, was two, three, even fourfold' is palpably nonsense when said of 1914, though true perhaps in 1917 when the monograph was written.

The fact seems to be that the Germans cannot understand defeat in war except on the premise that the victor had superiority of numbers. To show to what extent this creed obtains: in the late Dr Wylie's *Henry V*, vol II. page 216, will be found an account of a German theory, accepted by the well-known historian Delbrück, that the English won at Agincourt on account of superior numbers, although contemporary history is practically unanimous that the French were ten to one. Dr Wylie sums it up thus:

'Starting with the belief that the defeat of the French is inexplicable on the assumption that they greatly outnumbered the English, and finding that all contemporary authorities, both French and English, are agreed that they did, the writer builds up a theory that all the known facts can be explained on the supposition that the French were really much inferior to us in numbers ... and concludes that he cannot be far wrong if he puts the total number of French (the English being 6,000) at something between 4,000 and 7,000.'

It may not be out of place to add that a German Staff Officer captured during the Ypres fighting said to his escort as he was being taken away: 'Now I am out of it, do tell me where your reserves are concealed; in what woods are they?' and he refused to believe that we had none. Apparently it was inconceivable to the German General Staff that we should stand to fight unless we had superior numbers; and these not being visible in the field, they must be hidden away somewhere.

Further light on what the Germans imagined is thrown by prisoners, who definitely stated that their main attack was made south of Ypres, because it was thought that our main reserves were near ST JEAN, north-east of that town. From others it was gathered that what could be seen of our army in that quarter was in such small and scattered parties that it was taken to be an outpost line covering important concentrations, and the Germans did not press on, fearing a trap.

It is, however, possible that the German miscalculation of the number of formations engaged may not be altogether due to imaginary reserves, as regards the British Army. Before the war the Great General Staff knew very little about us. The collection of 'intelligence' with regard to the British Empire was dealt with by a Section known in the Moltkestrasse as the 'Demi-monde Section,' because it was responsible for so many countries; and this Section admittedly had little time to devote to us. Our organization was different from that of any of the great European armies. Their field artillery brigades contained seventy-two guns, whereas ours had only eighteen guns or howitzers; their infantry brigades consisted of two regiments, each of three battalions, that is six battalions, not four as in the original British Expeditionary Force. To a German, therefore, an infantry brigade meant six battalions, not four, and if a prisoner said that he belonged to the Blankshire Regiment, the German might possibly believe he had identified three battalions, whereas only one would be present. This is actually brought out on page 118, when the author speaks of the 1st Battalion of the King's (Liverpool) Regiment as the Königsregiment Liverpool, and indicates his ignorance of the British Army, when this single battalion engages the German Garde Regiment zu Fuss , by describing the fight not only as one of regiment against regiment, but as Garde gegen Garde (Guard against Guards).[3] Such is the fighting value of an English Line battalion. A victory over it is certainly claimed, but the significant sentence immediately follows: 'any further advance on the 11th November by our Guard troops north of the road was now out of the question.'

It may be as well to point out that the 'volunteers' who it is said flocked to the barracks to form the Reserve Corps XXII to XXVII were not all volunteers in our sense of the word. The General Staff only claims that 75 per cent. were untrained, a very different state of affairs from our New Armies, which had not 1 per cent. of trained soldiers. Many of the 'volunteers' were fully trained men liable to service, who merely anticipated their recall to the colours. It was well known before the war that in each army corps area Germany intended to form one 'Active' Corps and one or more 'Reserve' Corps. The original armies of invasion all contained Reserve Corps notably the IV Reserve of Von Kluck's Army, which marched and fought just as the active ones did. These first formed Reserve Corps were, it is believed, entirely made up of trained men, but those with the higher numbers XXII, XXIII, XXVI and XXVII, which appear in the Fourth Army, probably did contain a good percentage of men untrained before the war.

Ersatz divisions were formed of the balance of reservists after the Reserve divisions had been organized, and of untrained men liable for service. After a time the words 'Active,' 'Reserve,' and 'Ersatz' applied to formations lost their significance, as the same classes of men were to be found in all of them.

No attempt has been made to tone down the author's patriotic sentiments and occasional lapses from good taste; the general nature of the narrative is too satisfactory to the British Army to make any omissions necessary when presenting it to the British public.

German soldiers moving a giant howitzer to its concrete bed.

German captives marching on the final leg of the journey to the compound at Frith Hill, Camberley. Officers, to their disgust, received the same treatment as the rank and file.

German troops in their positions near Ypres during 1915 enjoying a captured copy of the *Daily Mail*.

Reinforcements for Ypres, soldiers of the Imperial German Army on the march through Belgium.

German officers oversee the test firing of a machine gun.

CHAPTER 8

ADOLF HITLER AT YPRES

One soldier serving in the ranks of the Imperial German Army was destined to become the most notorious man in history. Adolf Hitler was serving in the ranks of the 16th Bavarian Reserve Infantry Regiment, known as the List Regiment after its first commander. Hitler was to become very familiar with the distant aspect of the town of Ypres, his war started near the town in 1914 and four years later it would also end there in October 1918 when he was temporarily blinded by a British gas shell. Twenty four years later during one of his rambling monologues which were later collected together and published as *Hitler's Table Talk*, the Führer recalled the first tantalizing glimpse of the town which would remain within the grasp of the German armies but which would never fall to them. *'My first impression of Ypres was—towers, so near that I could all but touch them. But the little infantryman in his hole in the ground has a very small field of vision.'*

We are also fortunate that we also have Adolf Hitler's letter to Ernst Hepp which provides us with a surprisingly detailed account of the reality of service in a front-line unit during the early months of the Great War:

'Then morning came. We were now a long way from Lille. The thunder of gunfire had grown somewhat stronger. Our column moved forward like a giant snake. At 9am, we halted in the park of a country house. We had two hours' rest and then moved on again, marching until 8pm. We no longer moved as a regiment, but split up into companies, each man taking cover against enemy airplanes. At 9pm, we pitched camp. I couldn't sleep. Four paces from my bundle of straw lay a dead horse. The animal was already half decayed. Finally, a German howitzer battery immediately behind us kept sending two shells flying over our heads into the darkness of the night every quarter of an hour. They came whistling and hissing through the air, and then, far in the distance, there came two dull thuds. We all listened. None of us had ever heard that sound before. While we were huddled close together, whispering softly and looking up at the stars in the heavens, a terrible racket broke out in the distance. At first it was a long way off, and then the crackling came closer and closer, and the sound of single shells grew to a multitude, finally becoming a continuous roar. All of us felt the blood quickening in our veins. The English were making one of their night attacks. We waited a long time, uncertain what was happening. Then it grew quieter and at last the sound ceased altogether—except for our own batteries—which sent out their iron greetings to the night every quarter of an hour. In the morning we found a big shell hole. We had to brush ourselves up a bit, and about 10am there was another alarm and, a quarter of an hour later, we were on the march. After a long period of wandering about we reached a farm that had been shot to pieces and we camped here. I was on watch duty that night and, about one o'clock, we suddenly had another alarm; and we marched off at three o'clock in the morning. We had just taken a bit of food, and we were waiting for our marching orders, when Major Count Zech rode up: "Tomorrow we are attacking the English!" he said. So it had come

at last! We were all overjoyed; and after making this announcement, the Major went on foot to the head of the column.'

The 'English' which Major Count Zech was referring to consisted of elements of Worcester Regiment in position between the village of Gheluvelt and the town of Ypres. Also in the vicinity were some companies of the Scottish regular regiment, the renowned Black Watch. Although this was not a full scale battle it was to prove a bitterly fought encounter. Hitler only ever fought in two engagements and, not surprisingly, the events of October and early 1914 were destined to feature heavily in the pages of *Mein Kampf*.

The List Regiment had well and truly received its baptism of fire on 29th October 1914 and the casualties suffered by the List regiment in October 1914 were severe. Hitler's description of the regiment's first taste of combat confirms the ferocity of the engagement: '*And then followed a damp, cold night in Flanders. We marched in silence throughout the night and as the morning sun came through the mist an iron greeting suddenly burst above our heads. Shrapnel exploded in our midst and spluttered in the damp ground. But before the smoke of the explosion disappeared a wild 'Hurrah' was shouted from two hundred throats, in response to this first greeting of Death. Then began the whistling of bullets and the booming of cannons, the shouting and singing of the combatants. With eyes straining feverishly, we pressed forward, quicker and quicker, until we finally came to close-quarter fighting, there beyond the beet-fields and the meadows. Soon the strains of a song reached us from afar. Nearer and nearer, from company to company, it came. And while Death began to make havoc in our ranks we passed the song on to those beside us: Deutschland, Deutschland Über Alles, Über Alles In Der Welt.*'

Hitler and the List Regiment acquitted themselves well during the fight around Gheluvelt, but casualties, amounting to two thirds of the strength of the regiment, were very high – even by Great War standards. Hitler's description of the battle for Gheluvelt is detailed at great length in his letter to Ernst Hepp. The fight clearly made a huge impression on him and he went to some trouble to ensure that Herr Hepp had all of the details. The situation was fluid and confused, and although trenches were beginning to appear on the battlefield, this was one of the last occasions on the Western Front on which armies would manoeuvre in the open: '*Early, around 6am, we came to an inn. We were with another company and it was not till 7am that we went out to join the dance. We followed the road into a wood, and then we came out in correct marching order on a large meadow. In front of us were guns in partially dug trenches and, behind these, we took up our positions in big hollows scooped out of the earth; and waited. Soon, the first lots of shrapnel came over, bursting in the woods, and smashing up the trees as though they were brushwood. We looked on interestedly, without any real idea of danger. No one was afraid. Every man waited impatiently for the command: "Forward!" The whole thing was getting hotter and hotter. We heard that some of us had been wounded. Five or six men brown as clay were being led along from the left, and we all broke into a cheer: six Englishmen with a machine gun! We shouted to our men marching proudly behind their prisoners. The rest of us just waited. We could scarcely see into the steaming, seething witches' caldron which lay in front of us. At last there came the ringing command: "Forward!"*

We swarmed out of our positions and raced across the fields to a small farm. Shrapnel was bursting left and right of us, and the English bullets came whistling through the shrapnel; but we paid no attention to them. For ten minutes, we lay there; and then, once again, we were ordered to advance. I was right out in front, ahead of everyone in my platoon. Platoon-leader Stoever was hit. Good God! I had barely any time to think; the fighting was beginning in earnest! Because we were out in the open, we had to advance quickly. The captain was at the head. The first of our men had begun to fall. The English had set up machine guns. We threw ourselves down and crawled slowly along a ditch. From time to time someone was hit, we could not go on, and the whole company was stuck there. We had to lift the man out of the ditch. We kept on crawling until the ditch came to an end, and then we were out in the open field again. We ran fifteen or twenty yards, and then we found a big pool of water. One after another, we splashed through it, took cover, and caught our breath. But it was no place for lying low. We dashed out again at full speed into a forest that lay about a hundred yards ahead of us. There, after a while, we all found each other. But the forest was beginning to look terribly thin.

At this time there was only a second sergeant in command, a big tall splendid fellow called Schmidt. We crawled on our bellies to the edge of the forest, while the shells came whistling and whining above us; tearing tree trunks and branches to shreds. Then the shells came down again on the edge of the forest, flinging up clouds of earth, stones, and roots; and enveloping everything in a disgusting, sickening, yellowy-green vapor. We can't possibly lie here forever, we thought and, if we are going to be killed, it is better to die in the open. Then the Major came up. Once more we advanced. I jumped up and ran as fast as I could across meadows and beet fields, jumping over trenches, hedgerows, and barbed-wire entanglements; and then I heard someone shouting ahead of me: "In here! Everyone in here!" There was a long trench in front of me and, in an instant, I had jumped into it; and there were others in front of me, behind me, and left and right of me. Next to me were Württembergers, and under me were dead and wounded Englishmen.

The Württembergers had stormed the trench before us. Now I knew why I had landed so softly when I jumped in. About 250 yards to the left there were more English trenches; to the right the road to Leceloire was still in our possession. An unending storm of iron came screaming over our trench. At last, at ten o'clock, our artillery opened up in this sector. One—two—three—five—and so it went on. Time and again a shell burst in the English trenches in front of us. The poor devils came swarming out like ants from an ant heap, and we hurled ourselves at them. In a flash we had crossed the fields in front of us, and after bloody hand-to-hand fighting in some places, we threw [the enemy] out of one trench after another. Most of them raised their hands above their heads. Anyone who refused to surrender was mown down. In this way we cleared trench after trench.

At last we reached the main highway. To the right and left of us there was a small forest, and we drove right into it. We threw them all out of this forest, and then we reached the place where the forest came to an end and the open road continued. On the left lay several farms—all occupied—and there was withering fire. Right in front of us, men were falling. Our Major came up; quite fearless, and smoking calmly; with his adjutant, Lieutenant Piloty. The Major saw the situation at a glance, and ordered us to assemble, on both sides of the highway for an assault. We had lost our officers, and there were hardly any noncommissioned officers. So all of us, every one of us who was still walking, went running back to get reinforcements. When I returned the second time with a handful of stray Württembergers, the Major was lying on the ground with his chest torn open, and there was a heap of corpses all around him.

By this time, the only remaining officer was his adjutant. We were absolutely furious.

"Herr Leutnant, lead us against them!" we all shouted. So we advanced straight into the forest, fanning out to the left, because there was no way of advancing along the road. Four times we went forward, and each time we were forced to retreat. From my company, only one other man was left besides myself, and then he, too, fell. A shot tore off the entire left sleeve of my tunic but, by a miracle, I remained unharmed. Finally, at 2am we advanced for the fifth time; and this time, we were able to occupy the farm and the edge of the forest. At 5pm, we assembled and dug in, a hundred yards from the road. So we went on fighting for three days in the same way, and on the third day the British were finally defeated. On the fourth evening we marched back to Werwick. Only then did we know how many men we had lost. In four days our regiment consisting of thirty-five hundred men was reduced to six hundred. In the entire regiment there remained only thirty officers. Four companies had to be disbanded. But we were all so proud of having defeated the British!'

Despite all the inherent evils of the job, Hitler had a love of soldiering which never left him, but even wearing his most rose-tinted glasses, he must have known that his audience was unlikely to be taken in by a description of eager units advancing towards each other singing patriotic songs. It is certainly true that in the intensive battles of the early war units would sing a snatch of 'Der Wacht Am Rhein' which was the proscribed means of verbal recognition in the early stages of the war, but this activity had a distinct purpose. Hitler's less dramatic description of the withdrawal of the List Regiment from the line is much more convincing: *'After four days in the trenches we came back. Even our step was no longer what it had been. Boys of seventeen looked now like grown men. The rank and file of the List Regiment had not been properly trained in the art of warfare, but they knew how to die like old soldiers.'*

Adolf Meyer of the List Regiment writing in his diary recalled one of the defining moments of the battle. This was the instant when Colonel List was killed by a British shell. It is not surprising that in all the confusion of battle there are differing accounts of the death of the Colonel. According to Meyer, List was killed fighting in the very front ranks. His diary entry records the effects of the fighting: *'Only a few regiments have had to give such a heavy toll in blood in their first fight, the proud List Regiment had melted down to the strength of a battalion, the brave regimental leader, Colonel List, felled by a direct hit in the furthest forward line.'*

Hans Mend writing in his book, gives a completely different account of the circumstances of the Colonel's death. Mend was an eye witness and recalled how he was on his way to see Colonel List, who was then engaged in setting up headquarters in the recently captured Gheluvelt chateaux. As he approached the building Mend witnessed what he described as a 'three heavy English shells' crashing into the building.' According to Mend this was the real cause of the death of Colonel List: *'I could see nothing any more, and could no longer breathe for dust. Hearing cries of help coming from the chateaux, Mend rushed forward and was able to describe the scene as an eyewitness in which he attempted to assist in the rescue effort which was being performed by a group of Saxons, a few telegraph operators sprang immediately to the aid of the wounded. At once, one cried out: "The Bavarian colonel is also dead!" In my horror, I left my horse unattended, and sprang to the side of Colonel List, now covered by a tent flap. I lifted this away and saw that blood welled from his mouth. Our brave commander, who was a true leader of his troops, was no more.'*

On Sunday, 2nd August 1914, a twenty-five year old Adolf Hitler was amongst thousands of people gathered at the Odeonsplatz in Munich. The crowd joined in exuberant enthusiasm for the war and Heinrich Hoffman was on hand to record the scene. He later identified Hitler as a figure in the crowd.

Opposite: The earliest known photograph of *Regimentsordonnanzen* (Regimental Orderlies) and messengers Ernst Schmidt, Anton Bachmann and Adolf Hitler. Seated at Hitler's feet is the English Terrier named Foxl, who came to be Hitler's most treasured companion. The photograph was taken in April 1915 in Fournes.

Hitler with his comrades in September 1915, at the Regimental Command Post in Fromelles. Photograph by Hans Bauer: (Front row, left to right) Adolf Hitler, Josef Wurm, Karl Lippert, Josef Kreidmayer. (Middle row, left to right) Karl Lanzhammer, Ernst Schmidt, Jacob Höfele, Jacob Weiss. (Back row) Karl Tiefenböck.

The badly damaged town of Fromelles, where the Regimental Headquarters of the 16th RIR was situated from 17th March 1915 to 27th September 1916. Even in the rear areas, such as this, long-range shelling was a constant menace.

In this photograph taken at the beginning of September 1916, Hitler is seen alongside his colleagues and his faithful dog Foxl in the rear area at Fournes. (Front row, left to right) Adolf Hitler, Balthasar Brandmayer, Anton Bachmann, Max Mund. (Back row, left to right) Ernst Schmidt, Johann Sperl, Jacob Weiss and Karl Tiefenböck.

Orderly Sergeant Max Amann (left) pictured at La Bassée station in March 1917.

The conditions in the water-logged frontline trenches near Fromelles were appalling, as this photograph from May 1915 graphically demonstrates. The men of the 16th RIR lived and fought in these conditions.

Adolf Hitler in 1916 in the rear area at Fournes.

Adolf Hitler and Karl Lippert in mid-1915 in Fournes.

Adolf Hitler, then a battalion-messenger, seen in May 1915 with his rifle slung over his shoulder. Hitler was in the process of delivering a message. This photograph first appeared in the Official Regimental History of the 16th RIR.

Top, above and opposite top: Hitler, accompanied by Max Amann and Ernst Schmidt and aides, after the victory over France on 26th May 1940. The group were photographed on their tour to visit the positions they had occupied during the Great War in Flanders.

Hitler (left with helmet), and next to him Balthasar Brandmayer, pose for the camera in a bunker near the frontline section of Reincourt-Villers in September 1916.

Hitler with his comrades in May 1916 in Fournes: Balthasar Brandmayer (front), (left to right seated) Johann Wimmer, Josef Inkofer, Karl Lanzhammer, Adolf Hitler, (left to right standing) Johann Sperl, Max Mund.

Hitler with (right to left) Max Amann, Wehrmacht adjutant Gerhard Engel, Ernst Schmidt and adjutant Julius Schaub on 26th April 1940 at the same location in Fournes, some 24 years later.

Hitler on 26th October 1916, in the Prussian Association of the Red Cross hospital in Beelitz near Berlin, where he was brought after being wounded on 5th October 1916.

Hitler pictured in 1915.

Hitler pictured in 1919.